# IN PRAISE OF
# WHAT IF … YOU LIVED 300 YEARS?

"Paula's offering of this pioneering, mind-stretching concept was worth every moment of my time! Her book is filled with courage, tremendous curiosity, and desire for connection, humbleness, authenticity, and how important it is to accept responsibility for our life. I see how this 300-year mind set is a portal for the human species to become more loving and unified. We have learned how important resilience and adaptation are to making it through times that are turned upside down. Her questions for the reader's rumination are perfect!

What amazes me is how this idea came to her at such a young age. Plus, she knew instinctively that she was not limited by her life's circumstance. Having the insight to avoid the lure of a culturally acceptable career, she followed her inner guidance and made her way perfectly. She's definitely one of the wise ones! Read this book slowly and do the inner work. You'll witness your life's richness increase drastically."

— Laura Abernathy, Founder of the Tree of Life Sanctuary —

"Consider the perspective that most people have NOT considered...
We are living longer because of the medical miracles and the science for
maintaining our health. So, we must now learn to really live beyond what
was considered a normal lifespan. Paula Forget's book asks us how we can be
happy and productive after the accepted retirement age of 65 years.
How would our philosophy of living change to meet the additional decades
we have been potentially blessed to receive? Changing our mental attitudes,
changing our habits, changing our view of our relationships with work,
creativity, productivity, life satisfaction, and inter-personal relations need to
be considered. Paula's book offers examples of what may help to break us out
of out-dated ways of thinking. Do not let living longer sneak up on you!
Do not "settle" for a passive life if you want to be a vibrant contribution to
our world. Be better prepared for the best life possible as we move
into uncharted territory of longer, healthier lives."
— L. John Mason, Ph.D., Founder of the Stress Education Center —

"This book awakened me to adventures and
opportunities in life that are so easily overlooked.
In these pages I discovered that we don't grow old,
we just grow tired of playing the same game.
After reading this, I know that if I plan to be 300,
I can change my life as many times as I want."
— Bob Trask, Co-Founder of the ARAS Foundation —

# WHAT IF . . .
# YOU LIVED 300 YEARS?

*How to Live with Resilience in Changing Times*

## PAULA FORGET

**BOOKS OF LIGHT PUBLISHING**
BELLINGHAM, WA

# WHAT IF ... YOU LIVED 300 YEARS?
## How to Live with Resilience in Changing Times

**Paula Forget**

Books of Light Publishing
Bellingham, WA



Book design: Bob Paltrow Design
Book Illustrations: Paula Forget using Canva Graphic Design Content
Front cover photograph "Future" by RB Fried from Getty Images Signature and Canva
Printed in the United States of America

ISBN: 979-8218-24154-4

Library of Congress Control Number: 2023912731



www.ifyoulived300years.com

The primary cause of unhappiness

is never the situation

but your thoughts about it.

— ECKHART TOLLE —


Resilience is the process and outcome of adapting

to different or challenging life experiences, especially

through mental, emotional, and behavioral flexibility

and adjustment to external and internal demands.

— AMERICAN PSYCHOLOGICAL ASSOCIATION —

# CONTENTS

# INTRODUCTION

What if you could live 300 years healthy, vibrant, full of enthusiasm and curiosity, what would that be like for you? What dreams would you consider accomplishing? How would it change your perspective, moving into your future?

Let us examine how an event that occurred in my early 20s caused me to shift the way I viewed my life and the decisions I would make moving forward and developed in me an attitude of curiosity, wonder, and resilience.

Join me as we explore a life filled with possibilities, fateful and pragmatic, along with scientific discoveries that cause us to ponder what awaits us in the 21st century.

We all know that it is not likely today that any of us will live 300 years, yet approaching life as if we could, can give us a new view of the world. Advances in epigenetics indicate that future generations will live much longer than 100 years. For example, Dr. David Sinclair, of the Paul F. Glen Center for Biology of Aging Research at Harvard Medical School, has demonstrated how we can slow down, and even reverse, aging [1]. No one has had to really think about such longevity before! It used to be reserved to the realm of science fiction. We now have to consider our extended lives and how our vision of the future will change. With the current research in reverse aging (making an old organism young again), it may be possible to extend our lives beyond the eight or nine decades we are familiar with. Scientists from all over the world are studying our DNA and are close to making breakthroughs in slowing, and perhaps even reversing, the aging process.

Finding the genetic roots of disease, developing treatments, and perhaps even extending our lives, our future may look very different. We may be able to enjoy some of these advances in science and medicine in the near future.

If our lives were truly extended by an additional fifty or one hundred years, we could find many more applications of the wisdom we have gleaned along the way. As Dr. George Church, renowned American geneticist, stated, the objective is to "have the body and mind of a 22-year-old but the experience of a 130-year-old." This sounds ridiculously optimistic to me today, yet, who knows how our attitude and perspective can change, with new scientific discoveries! (2)

This book is not so much about the prospects of someday living to 300 or beyond, but of having the attitude that allows us to live a full life right now. I propose that approaching our futures with open minds can give us the ability to recognize the value of the opportunities that are there in every day. I will be presenting a point of view, developed after exploring the outlook of centenarians, of how to live with resilience in changing times.

When I was in my early 20s, I began to live my life as though I were going to live 300 years. I began to live my life large. I would think, for example, that if I lived 300 years, I would probably live in more than one town, city, or even country; I would have more than one career; I would need to be adaptable to change; I would need to be open to new experiences. Looking back today, I see that this approach has served me well.

This is a manual to help you develop a higher perspective of events happening in your life and your reactions to them and perhaps prepare you for the 21st century!

At the end of each chapter, will be some thoughts to reflect upon, allowing you to examine your own life, with a new perspective, moving forward.

Enjoy this whimsical approach to life!

✦　✦　✦

(1) (2) Sinclair, La Plante, "Lifespan, Why We Age and Why We Don't Have To".

# PART I

# THE FORMATIVE YEARS

IF YOU LIVED
300 YEARS . . .

IT WOULD CHANGE YOUR
PERSPECTIVE

# The 300 Year Attitude

What if you lived 300 years? How would it change your perspective? How would it change your life experience? This question began to evolve in me one day after reading conversations with centenarians. This is how it began.

When I was young, I was curious about people who lived to be 100 years old. I was interested in their view of the world and whether they had any wisdom to share from their lives. How was their world when they grew up in the mid-1800s? They surely had witnessed many social and technological changes. I wanted to learn how they had coped with these changes and how they now managed their daily lives.

To satisfy my curiosity, I went to the library and read books about centenarians. I learned that they were all healthy: otherwise, they wouldn't have lived that long. Of course, they may have had age-related decreases in previous ability; nonetheless, they were still actively engaged in life.

Many started their interviews by saying: "I worked hard all my life." Yes, most had been raised on farms. Farming was the most common occupation in the United States during the 19th century. The demands of running a farm promoted a strong ethic of hard work and discipline. Farm life involved long days of manual labor, tending to the fields and animals. Most things were homemade. Since there was no electricity, it was early to bed and early to rise for everyone. Families had to rely on each other. There was little social interaction in rural areas.

Later on, they may have moved to large towns to attend school or work new jobs. Over the years, they had witnessed wars and had lost friends. Most had married, raised families, and had outlived many of their own children. They were still active. They followed a daily routine with regular habits. Many loved to keep a garden. They were interested in other people and were social.

Some still lived independently; others lived in assisted-living homes. They were aware of current world events and stayed involved in their communities. They frequently attended luncheons and group gatherings, where they would socialize with friends of many ages.

Some had strong views and attitudes about their health. They knew what worked for them. No young doctor was going to tell them what they should and shouldn't be doing. As one elder said: "I've outlived almost everybody I know. You're not going to tell me this is bad for my health!" Yes, they were opinionated yet they were also flexible, resilient, and interested in the future.

Ella Mae Cheeks Johnson, social worker and civic leader, in her book It Is Well with My Soul: The Extraordinary Life of a 106-Year-Old Woman, shares her most important lessons: moderation, perseverance, patience, compassion and love, the ability to listen to different points of view, and most of all, the value of being useful to others. She notes that the lessons that we learn early in life are those that we share later with others. She recognizes that talking with her grandchildren has given her perspective on the revolution in thought and expectations that form the future.

✦   ✦   ✦

Reading about centenarians really impressed me, and I began to think of the lessons I could learn from them and how I could apply them to my life. I pondered, if I lived to be 100, how would my view of the world change? Moving forward from my early 20's, I mused . . . what if I lived to be 200? For some reason, that didn't feel long enough. Then I thought to myself, what if I lived 300 years . . . It felt right! Yes! If I lived 300 years, that would be a long time, and I would really have to learn to be adaptable and flexible!

As a form of play, I would begin to imagine. If I lived to be 300, I wouldn't hold a grudge against someone for that long: it would be senseless. I would have to get over my hurts and disappointments. It would be silly at the age of 150 or 200, to  look back and still be angry about a childhood disappointment like not getting chocolate ice cream on my fifth birthday, or my older brother grabbing one of my toys, and refusing to give it back to me. Of course, I could probably think of real hurts that I'd been carrying for years. I'd have to get over them! With that perspective, if I was 200 years old, I'd still have a lot of living ahead of me. So I'd tell myself, stop whining about that! At some point I would be forced to develop perspective, learn to forgive, and move on. After all, it all happened so long ago.

Remembering some difficult times in my life, I started to re-examine them with this new point of view.

When I began thinking that way, it opened my world. I saw a whole Earth filled with possibilities, with so much to explore and experience. After all, I thought, "It's a great big world out there!" If I lived 300 years, I may live in more than one country, I may have more than one job or career, and if my heart was broken, I may have more than one companion. I would have to learn to mature emotionally. Approaching life that way showed me how to live with curiosity, creativity, and resilience. I noticed time and again how this play with perspective helped me develop a broader view of events when the world appeared chaotic and unbalanced.

In the next chapters, I will share with you how events that occurred early in life shaped and changed me, and how the 300 year perspective gave me resilience.

✦   ✦   ✦

## CHAPTER 1 REFLECTIONS

Living as though you could experience 300 years would change your perspective of what is possible for you. It would open you up to almost unlimited opportunities. It would allow you to dream of a future filled with new energy, with room for growth and opportunity. It's a great big world out there!

**Look at your childhood. Are there disappointments that you are still carrying today?**

**What would it feel like if you could let go of resentments? What would change in your life?**

**Write one affirmation that you can adopt today that can move you forward to a life of curiosity, creativity, and resilience.**

✦ ✦ ✦

# Choices our Parents Make

# Choices our Parents Make

Our early childhood is often determined by the choices our parents make as to the circumstances of our births and where we live. We do not choose our names, the cultures where we are raised, our social standings, or our environments. We may grow up in a small town or large city, in a poor or affluent neighborhood, in a powerful nation or in a developing country, in times of peace or war, to a stable, loving family or one filled with strife and difficulties.

Change came early for me. I was born to a young, unmarried woman. She did not have the means to care for me. Soon after my birth, she placed me in a Catholic orphanage in Montreal, Quebec, Canada. The records note that she was very distraught at having to give me up but felt it was best and wished that I would be adopted by a mother and father who would love me. I hope, in turn, that she was able to move forward and live a happy and productive life.

I was fortunate to have been adopted soon after birth by a loving family who raised me and cared for me. I had a big brother who was five years older. My parents moved to St. Lambert, a new community on the banks of the St. Lawrence River, across the bridge from the vibrant, cosmopolitan city of Montreal. My first memory was looking out the window of my room and seeing a new school being built in the distance. Facing it was only a large field that stretched for almost a mile. There was a newly paved road in front of our house, with a row of new homes on each side. My father would take me to the new park close by, where there was still a natural pond. I loved to sit by the edge of the pond and play with frogs. When I was young, I loved nature and animals and going for long walks on wooded trails with my father.

My parents structured my formative years and instilled in me good values. I learned about rules. I was not allowed to cross the street. I was a curious child, so I would often walk out of the house without telling my mother and go explore the world within the confines of my neighborhood block. I gave my mother heart attacks when she'd realize that I was missing! I would walk out the door, turn right and then walk down the sidewalk to the corner, then return. The next time, I would do the same, and peek around the corner and see more homes and walk down that way, then turn back. Eventually I explored the entire perimeter, continuing to turn right at the next corner until I found myself back home. Often a friendly policeman in his patrol car would drive by, ask me my name, pick me up, and take me back home to my grateful mother. I must have been two or three years old then.

I was then taught to memorize my home address.

I don't know my exact age when my parents moved us back to Montreal. It may have been when my older brother started going to primary school. We moved to the west side of the island, in a house that was on a hill. No roller skates for me! Mom said it was too dangerous. Also, I was still forbidden to cross the street. There were too many cars in the city.

We moved several times again in Montreal, from one community to another. Every time, I would look back at the familiar house with its memories and say goodbye with a heavy heart, like saying farewell to a good friend, but I would soon adjust to my new home, as it became new surroundings to explore. Living in new neighborhoods taught me how to adapt to change.

I believe that moving often early in life, although difficult at times, provided me with the resilience to adjust to new, unfamiliar environments. If I lived 300 years, I would still want to explore more of this great world, with its beauty, variety of life, and surprises.

✦　✦　✦

# CHAPTER 2 REFLECTIONS

We do not control the circumstances of our early childhood. Many decisions are made for us. Let us examine here our early lives and how these events have formed us to be the person we are today.

Briefly answer. We will have time to examine these issues in detail later.

**What choices were made for you in your early years of life?**

***What qualities did your parents (or guardians) have?***
***What values did they instill in you?***

***Did you grow up in the same town you were born in,***
***or did you move around?***

***How did it affect you?***

✦　✦　✦

# The Early Choices We Make

# CHAPTER 3
# The Early Choices We Make

When people asked me what I wanted to do when I grew up, I would tell them that I wanted to be a farmer. Being a city girl from Montreal, I'm sure that must have sounded funny to my parents. Of course, I had no thought of how much work was involved; I just saw myself surrounded by animals. Eventually, I lived in the country and in smaller towns, too, where I could be closer to nature; that I will share later.

I also loved the arts. I would spend hours drawing and coloring. My parents recognized that I had a natural aptitude and encouraged the fine arts, along with music and dance.

Although I studied piano for several years, I really concentrated on dance. Early on, my parents noticed that I would naturally stand on the tips of my toes as I mimicked dancing, so they signed me up for ballet school. It lifted my heart as I imagined myself as a bird, gracefully gliding across the dance floor. I appeared on stage in recitals at our town hall, and my parents took me to see a performance by the famous

Russian Bolshoi Ballet at Place des Arts. I studied ballet for ten years, starting at the age of three.

Then when I was thirteen years old, a scout from the New York City Ballet approached my parents and shared his interest in having me move to New York and join their school to further my training and eventually become part of their troupe. Sadly, my parents were experiencing financial difficulties at that time, so they decided to end my dance classes. (There may also have been other reasons for making that decision. It was an early age for me to choose a career that may be short-lived and prone to injuries. I would have had to move away from my family, which would have also been challenging for my parents. I don't think they were ready to see me leave home quite yet.)

 I didn't find out until my early twenties of this lost opportunity. In the meantime, I was broken-hearted. Giving up ballet was devastating to me at the age of 13. For years after, I could not even watch performances on television. In those days, a parent's decision was final, and that's how things were to be.

I wish I had the Great-Big-World perspective then.

An important event occurred around that time. It may have been a year or so later. I was sitting in my room crying. Normally, at home I was expected to behave as though I was always happy. I was raised in the British authoritarian model—loving and strict. To voice a strong opinion, to cry, or to be insubordinate would bring great disapproval from my parents. I always knew that I was very sensitive. I would often think, "why am

I SO SENSITIVE?" It was just how I was. I didn't blame anyone. But I developed the habit of saving all my crying to the end of the day, when I was alone. Then I would cry.

That particular evening, I was home alone in my room, and I felt so sad that I went to the bathroom, took a full bottle of aspirin and swallowed them. It wasn't something that I had contemplated doing before. It was just spontaneous, without thought.

Immediately after I did it, I thought to myself, "that is the stupidest thing that I have ever done! I will never allow anyone or anything to make me feel that bad ever again!" And in that instant, I decided to take personal responsibility for my feelings and actions and what I was going to do with my life.

It was a huge decision. I was going to be accountable for myself. Luckily, I was not harmed by the aspirins. Now, moving forward, I observed my feelings and reactions. I learned not to blame anyone or anything for them and instead, turned the focus on myself. How could I better move forward now? How would I deal with my sensitive nature? I had to own it.

Looking back at that moment today, I realize that it was a gift that helped me develop a proactive approach to my life. I instinctively knew that I was not limited by circumstance and that there's a Great Big World out there and I'm going to get some of it. My life was in my hands.

# Chapter 3 Reflections

As children, we enjoy playing carelessly along. It is a time in our lives when we discover the things we like to do, spending long hours occupied in those activities. Later on, a life path is chosen by us or by circumstance. Let us examine our dreams and what really inspires and ignites us.

**What did you like to spend hours doing as a child?**

**What did you want to be when you grew up?**

*What decision did your parents make when you were a child that you resented? Did that resentment benefit your life, or did it cause damage to your relationship with your parents?*

*Looking back at your formative years—looking at what you view as good and what you view as bad—how would you use these events as learning experiences moving into the future?*

◆　◆　◆

# LEARNING ABOUT OTHER CULTURES

# CHAPTER 4
# Learning About Other Cultures

Growing up in the cosmopolitan city of Montreal exposed me to people of many cultures. In school, I enjoyed stories and perspectives from my classmates: a girl raised in India telling me she once had pet tigers as a child; another from the Ukraine, proudly showing the finely detailed traditional needle-point designs on her blouse; a boy from Lebanon who spoke strongly about what friendship meant to him, saying, "I would DIE for my friend!" as we shuddered meekly, "Why would you have to die?" I had a friend from Africa who feared ghosts and spirits. He told me stories about how they roamed through his village and visited people's homes. Hmmm . . . I wondered about that. What were they doing there?

I grew up in an atmosphere of brotherhood. The Canadian Prime Minister at that time was Pierre Elliott Trudeau, and he promoted "Unity in Diversity!" One of the highlights of my youth was Expo 67, the World's Fair with the theme "Man and His World." Sixty-two countries from all over the world attended and shared a taste of the best they had to offer.

There were so many inspiring exhibits, some from rich countries, displaying their great wealth, others from struggling nations in the grips of poverty, still standing proud in their hope for the future.

The Swiss pavilion displayed dazzling watches encrusted with jewels. The United States presented Buckminster Fuller's forty-story Biosphere geodesic dome, with models of satellites and an actual space capsule and rockets. The French Pavilion was a dazzling eight-story architectural structure of concrete and steel, with shimmering aluminum fins, crowned with a rooftop terrace that offered an exceptional view of the entire exhibition. The interior displayed its cultural and technological advances, with electronic lights and ultra-modern music.

Other countries, such as Mauritius and Ethiopia, had more modest displays, depicting the flora and fauna, art, and histories of their people.

The Expo provided me with perspective of my place in the world. Living 300 years would help me realize even more how similar we are in our common aspiration for a good life and the love we hold for those dear to us.

✦  ✦  ✦

I had developed an interest in traveling. I loved to read about faraway places and cultures. After high school, as part of an exchange work program, I had the opportunity to live in Europe for a few months. Through Manpower, I was offered employment in Brussels, Belgium, working in a commercial laundry. It would give me the opportunity to explore the country and experience life in Europe. My parents took care of making the arrangements, and off I went to Belgium at the age of seventeen. The Great Big World awaited me!

During the long flight to Belgium, I reflected on what was awaiting me in this foreign country. It was my first time living away from home. I was excited by my new sense of freedom. At the same time, my future felt like a blank slate. I was moving forward into the unknown.

When I arrived, I met my Manpower representative, who gave me specifics of where I was going to live and my employer's address. I felt reassured knowing that I could rely on him during my stay.

I then went to the rooming house where arrangements had been made for me. I had a small room above a bakery. It had a window, a small bed, a nightstand, and an armoire where I could hang my clothing. Looking out the window, I could see the alley that ran behind the store. I could see the neighbors' backyards, where they had gardens with flowers and small vegetable patches. It all looked quite quaint. Then I decided to go exploring.

I familiarized myself with the city's transit system. Not having a car, I would be taking the bus to work. I took a taxi to the main bus terminal and picked up several bus schedules. From there, I began touring the city. I looked out the buses' window, gazing at the old-world architecture of the buildings and the people walking down the street and felt the atmosphere of this new country.

For a moment, I felt a tinge of insecurity being in this new environment. I wondered about my personal safety. I was surrounded by new unknowns.

I then decided that I would not live in fear. Looking at the people who walked by, I told myself that they were not afraid to live here, and I would not be afraid either! I decided that living life in fear was not an option for me. I then felt confident and was excited to begin my adventure. Looking back at that moment now, I realize that it helped form my attitude. If I lived 300 years, I could not live in fear!

On my first day of work at the commercial laundry I got dressed and went downstairs, where a sweet roll waited for me from the bakery. I went back to my room and looked over my bus schedule as I ate my breakfast. I would board the bus a block down the street, then transfer to another that would take me straight to the laundry.

I went down to the corner and soon my bus appeared. On the bus, I watched as the city woke up and people were busy getting to work. Shops were opening their doors and outdoor cafes were setting up for the day. I got off the bus at the place where I was going to meet my transfer. Sitting on the bench next to the stop, I had used the 35 minute wait to look at my surroundings. It was a busy part of town with a mix of commercial and residential buildings. Next to me was a small hotel. I then noticed an older gentleman sitting at an outside table eating his breakfast and reading a newspaper. I thought to myself, I wouldn't mind having a hearty breakfast in the morning! The next morning, I ordered the same breakfast. It had coffee, fruit, eggs, potatoes and two slices of bread, and a thick slice of cheese. I would wrap the bread and cheese and save the sandwich for lunch. Every morning, I would watch the older gentleman, sitting leisurely, reading his morning paper.

I boarded my next bus and soon arrived at the commercial laundry. I was greeted by the plant manager, who gave me a tour of the facilities and introduced me to my coworkers. The company washed uniforms for large companies such as hotels, butcher shops, and gas stations. My job was simple: using a small nozzle gun, I would stand in place blowing air into uniform pockets, getting rid of dirt and dust before they were laundered. I had a break in the morning, and a break for lunch, and another break in the afternoon.

I had never worked in that environment before. It was repetitive and fairly mindless. I knew that it was a temporary job for me—only for the summer—then I would return to Canada. In the meantime, I had the opportunity to experience life in

Europe. I watched my coworkers, especially those who were much older than I and wondered if this kind of work was all that was available for them to do. I wondered about their lives and stories. I did not know then that a few decades later, I would choose factory work to supplement my income from time to time. At that young age though, I swore to myself that when I returned home, I would find an interesting and rewarding career for myself. After all, I had my whole life ahead of me.

If I had had my 300-year attitude at that time, I would have viewed this job as part of an ongoing learning experience, one of many to come.

While in Europe, I visited France, Italy, and Holland. What an eye-opening experience it was to visit countries with so much history! Each was different, with its unique language, food, and customs. Their cultures had learned to adapt to so many changes over the centuries, surviving wars and political insurrections. I admired the resilience of the European people.

# CHAPTER 4 REFLECTIONS

During our lives so far, we have probably encountered people from a variety of customs, traditions, and points of view. It deepens our understanding of each other, helping us realize that our differences add to the richness of our world, while at the same time, we have much in common.

**Fear of the unknown can prevent us from moving forward or enjoying life. Although it is wise to use caution when undertaking new experiences, allowing ourselves to encounter new environments can allow us to learn and grow in new ways. If you lived 300 years, how would you deal with fear?**

**Do you have friends from different cultures than your own?**
**What have you learned from them?**

**Have you traveled to areas that are different from where you grew up? What were those areas like?**

**Have you had to overcome a fear of traveling or discovering a new environment?**

**How did you overcome it?**

✦ ✦ ✦

# If you lived 300 years. . .

you would choose many life paths

# CHAPTER 5
# Choosing Life Paths

When I returned from Belgium, I was ready to go to college. I had so many interests that it was hard to choose a major. I loved the arts, I loved observing people, and I also had an interest in science. I liked to understand how things work. Most of all though, I was curious about an odd topic that had intrigued me for years. Telepathy.

In my early teens, I noticed that I would have dreams about my future. I would often dream of everyday events, nothing special. No earthquakes, no end of the world or cataclysmic events. Then, when one of these everyday events happened, I would experience a flash of recognition, and would remember when I had dreamed of the event. So, I started to call them flashes. I became fascinated with how the element of time played into the events. I wondered how I could know of an event before it happened.

It happened to me so often that I wanted to study the science that would help me discover its workings. I believed that if I understood how it occurred, I could teach others how to have those experiences. When I prepared to go to college, I wondered which branch of science to pursue. Would the answers I was seeking be found in psychology, biochemistry, or physics? Precognition was a new area of research at that time, and there was no path of study at the universities that I was aware of. That kind of research was purely experimental and not part of the mainstream.

I entered college and decided to focus on psychology and fine art. After a year, I realized that much of psychology was based on behavioral theory. With no direct route into rigorous scientific research into precognition and its relationship with time, I felt uncertain about studying for years towards a PhD degree in a field that may not lead me to the answers I was seeking. I decided that I could do the research on my own and maybe someday write my own findings. Although I enjoyed fine art, it did not stimulate my curiosity enough to pursue it further.

Instead, I left college for now, and decided to travel and see the world. I had spent years reading about other cultures and far-away places. I had spent a short time in Europe and now wanted to see more of this great world. So, I joined the airlines and began my adult life.

Yes, if I lived 300 years, I would choose many life paths. This was only the beginning of many more careers to follow, which would later bring me back to some of my original interests.

✦   ✦   ✦

# CHAPTER 5 REFLECTIONS

If you lived with the 300 years attitude, you may choose many life paths. As you change and grow, you may develop new interests. Those that you choose early in life may evolve.

**What were your career interests early in life?**

**What did you find interesting about them?**

**Did you have to make a choice of which path to follow? How did you decide?**

✦　✦　✦

# PART II

# LIFE'S UNFOLDMENT

IF YOU LIVED
300 YEARS . . .
YOU MAY HAVE
MORE THAN
ONE JOB OR
CAREER

# Developing Through Different Careers

After college, I worked for a Canadian airline as a reservation agent. I would have loved to have been a flight attendant, but I knew that it was not for me. Although I loved to fly, I had a tendency to motion sickness. When I was younger, I could not go on rides at amusement parks, or take long car trips, or fly in an airplane without experiencing that queasy feeling in my stomach. But I still loved to travel! I enjoyed the benefits my job offered. It provided me with discounted airfare that I used to plan short, monthly trips to British Columbia, Hawaii, and Mexico, visiting friends and exploring new shores.

The friends that I had at the time worked in the travel industry. They were open-minded and adventurous. They also had many interests and loved to learn new things. That is how I met my husband. He was American and was visiting Canada during the winter. He enjoyed winter sports like skiing and sledding. We enjoyed long walks in the country and talked about the things that mattered to us. Then when spring arrived, it was time for him to return to the United States. We did not want to be apart, so we decided to get married, and I moved to the United States.

While settling into married life, I took a job working for a large Insurance firm. I went to school and took specialized insurance classes, expanding my knowledge of the industry. I can't say that it was a thrill for me. It was dry, somewhat boring, and lacked creativity. I did, however, develop an appreciation for legal principles and learn to think with precision. Every word was weighed and measured. I am glad to have gained the flexibility to think from many perspectives. I realized that people are unique in the ways that they think, and it has given me an appreciation for the different perspectives people have. Yes, if I lived 300 years, it would not be the last time that I had been surprised by different points of view.

For several years, my husband and I conducted our own psychical research. We read about some of the investigations taking place at universities around the world. We repeated some studies in telepathy that had been conducted at Duke University by Dr. J. B. Rhine, founder of the parapsychology lab. We also standardized Kirlian photography that measures coronal discharges, as a diagnostic tool to examine cyclical changes in the body. We also learned how to control our brainwaves with biofeedback, a skill that was useful when I began practicing meditation to attain a tranquil state of mind.

Because of our youth, inexperience, and lack of funds, we were not able to continue our work, although it gave us direct insight into the more subtle facets of our natures. But there was still the elusive aspect of time. These experiments still did not explain how the element of time seemed to be absent during telepathy and precognition.

If I lived 300 years, I told myself, maybe I would solve the mystery. I had to believe that someday, someone would stumble upon the answer.

After an 8-year career in Insurance, I was ready to move on and do something else. Something more challenging. After all, if I "lived 300 years" I wouldn't want to do the same thing the whole time.

I developed through different careers. For example, I decided that I would overcome my shyness. Although I was adventurous, I was also timid around people. I was able to present an outgoing appearance of ease, yet inside I felt uncomfortable. I decided to face it head-on.

I challenged myself by working for one of the employment agencies whose services I had used during my insurance career. Often, when I was working for large insurance firms, the opportunities for advancement may have been limited. A promotion may have had to wait until someone finally retired. I was not going to wait! So, I had hired the services of employment agencies to find the openings I was seeking and was able to progress in my career.

I worked for a year at the employment agency, interviewing a large number of applicants from various backgrounds in person and contacted employers in many fields. Sometimes I would meet up to twenty people a day. I loved speaking with diverse people. Taking the focus off myself helped me overcome my shyness.

An important insight I gained from meeting people at the employment agency was that the most successful of them had developed their natural aptitudes and used them in their career. More than having formal education, encouraging their natural talents is what allowed them to thrive. For example, I noticed that successful salespeople had a natural ability to relate with people, tell stories, and communicate ideas easily. It was as though they had been selling their whole lives! They didn't learn it from reading a book or taking special classes on how to make friends and influence people. Successful accountants on the other hand, were naturally focused, disciplined, and thorough. I sensed that they were that way in everything they did. I remembered this important lesson later in my life when I realized the value in developing my artistic talents.

To continue challenging myself to overcome my shyness, I then began to work for a hotel. I was meeting the traveling public, felt a kinship with them through remembering my trip to Europe, and loved to direct them to local attractions and restaurants. I enjoyed meeting a variety of people and cared about their well-being. I eventually progressed into management.

The way I overcame fears and insecurities and was able to move forward was by developing my "if I lived 300 years" optimistic attitude. There would always be another opportunity to learn to do better.

✦ ✦ ✦

# CHAPTER 6 REFLECTIONS

When we are young, events seem to move quickly. We often graduate from school, begin a job or career, move away from home. It can feel like a tumultuous time. If we lived with the "300 years" attitude, we would stop, take a breath, and realize that these changes only prepare you for what is to come later.

**What changes occurred to you in your early 20s?**

**Did they direct you into various jobs or careers?**

**How were you transformed by these changes?**

✦  ✦  ✦

If you lived 300 years. . .
you may go back to school many times,
learn new things, develop new skills,
discover new hobbies.

# Using New Skills

The world has kept changing throughout the years, and I have had to keep up with it. After all, in 300 years, the world will not wait for me! I realized that I needed to take classes in computer technology: social media, web design and marketing. The artist in me felt the need to take classes in video production and editing. I loved to dabble in a variety of creative media. I also taught myself graphic design and advertising. These were all necessary tools of my work, as new technologies emerged quickly.

✦　✦　✦

I took courses out of interest and sometimes necessity. I enrolled at my local college and registered for an automotive class. I wanted to know how to do general maintenance and repairs on my car. I realized that, since I would probably own one for the rest of my life, I may as well learn how it worked!

At the time, I owned a sports car, a Mazda RX-7, with a Chevy Chevelle V-8 engine under the hood. It was a retired race car. I owned it not so much to drive fast, but because I loved how it responded. When I pressed my foot on the gas, it went! I could even accelerate going uphill! It also made a wonderful vroom sound when I started it. It was a lot of fun to own.

We buy cars for many different reasons and uses in our lives. For example, at a young age, our first car may have been an old Volkswagen with many dings on it and a not-so-perfect paint job. It got us out of the house and gave us a new sense of independence. A few years later, we may have bought a sports car. It was fun, fast, and an extension of our free spirits. Then, when we settled down and had a family, we may have transitioned to a minivan.

During my career evolution into stained glass, I gave up my sports car for a more utilitarian vehicle. If I lived 300 years I would surely own many cars for many purposes. If I had a flat tire, I would simply say, "If I lived 300 years, it wouldn't be the last time that I will have a flat tire," and laugh.

I thought of many people who had learned new skills and developed new professions later in life. They had not been afraid of walking away from the familiar and trying something new. I told myself, if I lived 300 years, I would also undoubtedly begin new endeavors. It is never too late to develop new interests.

For example, Bob Ross spent twenty years in the air force. After he retired, he taught himself to paint and became a painting teacher at 41 years of age. He became popular on his PBS TV show.

Laura Ingalls Wilder, who wrote the *Little House on the Prairie* series, published her first book at the age of 65.

Julia Child, the well-known chef, was first a copywriter, and then worked in the intelligence field during World War II. She later went to cooking school and wrote her first cookbook at the age of 49.

Colonel Sanders was 65 when he started Kentucky Fried Chicken.

Grandma Moses didn't seriously paint until she was 76 years old and was a painter for the next 25 years.

I recently received word from my hairdresser, who had practiced her profession for twenty-five years. She was leaving and beginning her studies in dentistry. At first, I was happy for her. Equally though, I was disappointed to hear that I would no longer have my favorite hairdresser. Oh noooo! After six years, I would have to find a new one! That is when I reminded myself that she was not the first hairdresser I had loved and, if I lived 300 years, I would surely have many more. After all, every time I moved, I found a new, awesome, and talented hairdresser.

# CHAPTER 7 REFLECTIONS

Having a curious mind drives us to explore our world, develop new ideas, and discover how things work. You never know where these new insights may lead you. It is never too late to begin a new endeavor.

**What interests have you explored?**

**Have those interests stimulated your creativity?**

**What enjoyment have you gained from developing your interests?**

✦　✦　✦

The Arts

# CHAPTER 8
# Now, the Arts

When I was close to 40 years of age, I decided to follow the example of my employment agency clients and pursue one of my natural talents: the arts. Since I had a talent for drawing and painting using many media, I created an art portfolio and started a new career. I marketed my talents, first finding individual clients. Then I co-founded a new art co-op in a small town in northern Florida. Along with a handful of artists, we restored an old building and created a gallery where area artists could display their works. It became a hub for the arts in the community. We organized events for the community by holding art shows, theatre, and musical presentations in the town center. I created Christmas displays along Main Street during the holidays, produced art for community fundraisers, promoted our county at the Florida State Fair, and eventually gained recognition for my works. It was still difficult to make a good income creating art, and I worked extra jobs on the side to sustain myself.

My first big break was when I applied for a position in an art studio in Gainesville, Florida as a studio artist. I walked in with my art portfolio, with examples of the variety of media I had used: drawing, painting with oils, acrylics, watercolors, pastels, sculpture, and collages. They asked me if I had ever worked with an airbrush. Yes, I had one and I had used it to create posters and paint fabrics. I was hired. My new job was to paint limited editions of sculptures. This would be different than painting on a flat surface. I had to be mindful of the entire form as I sprayed the paint along its face. They were sculptures of wildlife and Native American people. The art pieces were then sold across the United States in specialty shops. (During a brief visit, I once saw the pieces displayed in a gallery on the Fisherman's Wharf in San Francisco). Although I did not have a formal education or a degree in fine art, I was recognized for my talent. It was all that I needed. The rest, I taught myself.

I continued my involvement with the art co-op on the weekends. One day, the Director of the Tourist Development Council, for whom I had created some displays depicting our county for the Florida State Fair, referred me to a stained- glass studio that was looking for a designer. They dealt predominantly with churches. These were large projects. They had me do a sketch as a test, to see if I might be able to transfer my skills to stained glass. They liked the result and forwarded the sketch to a studio in Nashville, Tennessee, that specialized in new churches and restoration of historic windows. I had never worked with glass, and I knew that I had much to learn.

The Nashville Studio hired me as a designer of church windows. I learned how to build leaded windows, then became a glass painter, using vitreous paints to restore antique windows. It was a wonderful experience! I never could have imagined that someday I would be working with a team of accomplished artisans, producing large works that would inspire people for years to come.

A few years later, I started my own stained-glass business, creating and restoring windows for private homes and businesses. I also taught art classes to groups, introducing them to the medium of stained glass.

◆　◆　◆

I was still hungry for new ways to express my artistic talents. One day, I saw a sign in front of another art studio on my daily route, and I stopped by to see what kind of projects they were involved with. This led me to a new artistic direction.

This studio had been founded by a former engineer from Disney's production studios. Now he was involved in creating displays and exhibits for museums and designing and building water features for distinctive homes. I wanted to be part of his team! This would allow me to explore new avenues, working on projects that I never would have dreamed of. I loved the variety of media and environments these studios offered. We produced displays for the new Mariners' Museum in Newport News, Virginia. We even built part of a battleship! How fun is that?! We also created the interior displays for the new Visitor Center at Hoover Dam, with dioramas depicting its construction.

Yes, using my natural talents had indeed led to a successful 20-year art career.

If we lived the 300 years attitude, it would undoubtedly transform our perspective regarding how we choose to mold our identities. What fills our souls as we live life in a meaningful way? Our life purposes may grow, mature, and come to crossroads where we choose new paths to follow.

We may focus on more than one career. After all, we each have many talents and abilities and are able to develop skills yet to be discovered. Our interests may change and new possibilities may present themselves. To explore a new career could provide us with a new level of challenges, growth, and satisfaction. In the future, we also may find that familiar jobs have evolved along with new technologies. We will find new excitement in these new opportunities.

✦　✦　✦

# CHAPTER 8 REFLECTIONS

Have you ever found yourself at a crossroads where you had to choose a new path to follow? We often find ourselves at a junction, a turning point in our lives, when we feel drawn into a new direction. Sometimes, we may feel that there is something inside ourselves that needs to be expressed. If you lived with the 300 years attitude, you would know that it may happen more than once in your long life.

✦  ✦  ✦

*How do you approach a crossroads in your life?*
*Is there one that comes to mind?*

*How did it make you feel?*

**What did you learn from your decision?**

✦　✦　✦

# DEALING
## with
# CHANGE

# Dealing with Change

Sometimes, unexpected events occur to change our plans. During the economic downturn of 2008, people were afraid of losing their homes. Financial uncertainty caused people to hold on to their funds until better days returned.

I had to look for new sources of income besides stained glass and fine art.

My search led me down a surprising path. I answered a non-specific job posting stating that needed "a compassionate person." I thought to myself, "I'm a compassionate person! I love people!" During the interview, I soon realized that I was being informed about employment at a funeral home/cemetery. My first thought was "No! That is not for me. I am a bright, cheerful person who loves life." Well, after reflection, I decided to take it on and see if it was a fit. I never thought that I would use my caring attitude for people, and my attention to detail, to work at a cemetery handling Family Services and attending to the needs of families who had lost a loved one.

I found many similarities with my hospitality experience that translated well into this profession. One of my responsibilities had been to work with groups attending events. Often, a family was making arrangements for family members attending a college graduation, wedding, or special event. They would be arriving from out-of-town, not knowing where to go, except for an address of where they would be staying and the location of the event. It was sometimes a chaotic time for them, and my job was to make their stay a smooth and comfortable experience, while also providing them directions to local restaurants and points of interest.

Working at the cemetery was similar. I would meet with the family at the time of a death and would go over the details of the arrangements they requested regarding where the church service or memorial would be held, along with information about the elements of the service, the location of the burial at the cemetery, and signing the state's required legal forms. About a month after the funeral, I would visit the family and provide them with bereavement material, including the names of local groups where they could receive emotional support. I would let them know that they did not have to go through their loss alone. I felt that the human contact was meaningful and personally rewarding.

During another lean time, I took on caregiving for a homecare agency. They needed a kind and compassionate caregiver to assist their clients. I had loved working with people and cared about their well-being. I started as homemaker and companion, moved on to providing personal care, then worked with people who suffered from dementia and Alzheimer's. I also worked in the office as a scheduler, being the liaison between the client and caregiver, and also assisted human resources in screening prospective caregivers. Working with an agency that provided individualized care and attention to a population that is often forgotten helped me develop a deeper sense of purpose.

I have been able to transfer my skills to many different occupations, when needed. During another period of transition, I used my stained-glass soldering skills in an industrial shop that manufactured dental equipment, soldering electronic components onto circuit boards. Years later, during an annual visit with my dental hygienist, she mentioned that she would be using the Cavitron Ultrasonic Scaler on my teeth. I had not heard that term in years and told her that I used to fabricate them.

Looking at a future filled with possibilities has kept me enthusiastic and eager to try new things, with my "if I lived 300 years" attitude.

I have also thought about the possibilities that today's younger generation will encounter if they live in a world of extended lifespans. How will they adapt to change? How will they view their own mortality? With time, will they become wiser? Will they want to pass on their life experiences, as they also learn new ways of living?

# Chapter 9 Reflections

Sometimes, circumstances require that we change course, that we explore new paths. Learning to develop curiosity can lead us to a life with resilience.

**What surprising events have caused you to re-examine your life goals?**

**How did you deal with the changes?**
**What lessons did you learn moving forward?**

**Are there things you might want to change today?**

**What careers would you choose if you could live 300 years?**

✦  ✦  ✦

# If you lived 300 years...

you would feel a spectrum of emotions
through life experiences

# CHAPTER 10
# Your Emotional Palette

How broad is your Emotional Palette? Do you resort back to a handful of habitual responses? Sometimes we stay stuck in familiar and safe behavioral patterns. We may avoid unfamiliar experiences, being afraid of feeling vulnerable facing the unknown. By broadening our Emotional Palette, we also deepen our understanding of life and our relationships.

✦ ✦ ✦

When I was younger, I was not permitted to play with roller skates. My mother was protective of me and, since our family lived on a hill, thought it was too dangerous. So, I just found many other ways of amusing myself.

Years after I had moved out, when I was busy working long hours and needed a break, I decided that I wanted to do something different on my upcoming day off. I wanted to try something new, something that would be fun and challenging at the same time. I decided to go roller skating!

On my next day off, I went down to my local roller-skating rink, and I rented a pair of roller skates. Now, I used to ice skate. Growing up in Canada, all children are fitted with ice skates from the time they can walk. It's a Canadian thing. I remember that my first pair was the two-blade skates that you tie on to your boots, and then later, when I could keep my balance, I got the single-blade skates.

I assumed that roller skates were not that different.

I got onto the rink. I immediately realized that unlike ice skates, roller skates didn't have metal edges. I had no way of controlling them. They just rolled! I hung onto the side of the rink, trying to get a sense of how to skate with them. Meanwhile, families were there with their children and there was a birthday party gathering down at one end of the rink. They were all confidently skating, having a great time. Even little children were flying right by me!

I let go of the side of the rink and started to slowly glide across the floor. Remembering my ice-skating skills, I tried to apply them to this new medium. I just didn't know how to stop or slow down. I headed to an area of the rink where there weren't any people and experimented with different ways to maneuver myself along. I watched from a distance as all these little children were now doing the bunny hop along with a parent, singing and enjoying their birthday party. Oh well, I guess it takes a grown-up to make roller skating difficult.

Even though I was not good at it, I had fun trying something new. It was my afternoon great adventure. I had been to a new place and done something I had never done before. I smiled when remembering it later when I was back at work.

✦ ✦ ✦

# CHAPTER 10 REFLECTIONS

We often respond to the world in predictable, habitual ways, which have become our emotional set-points. We are in a comfortable place within ourselves. Maintaining a status quo does not stimulate personal growth. The more you know, the more you can do, and the more you can enjoy life.

We are often faced with change in our lives. How we learn to adapt and move on will determine the quality of our life experiences. Having to face fear and uncertainty requires courage and resilience. It does get easier, the more you practice challenging yourself. You develop self-confidence from past accomplishments, knowing that even small achievements are a mark of your ability to learn new things.

**Looking at a normal day, what habitual emotions do you feel?**

***What attitudes do you carry that determine your daily set-point?***

***What can you do to expand your Emotional Palette?***

✦   ✦   ✦

# If you lived 300 years . . .

you would have to overcome many of your fears

# Overcoming Fear

Fear is probably the greatest roadblock to experiencing life fully. Uncertainty, lack of self-confidence, and obsessive and unreasonable thoughts of danger and apprehension can keep us trapped in a contracted and withdrawn state of being. It is important to approach the world with healthy caution, but it must be balanced with an openness to experience life. If you lived 300 years, you would not want to live life locked in your room! The sun is calling you out to a new day!

Some people love roller coasters, with the thrill and excitement of speed and movement. Others may prefer calm. Is risk-taking part of your character? Do you get bored when sitting still? Both types of people can learn from experiencing the other. A calm person can discover the stimulating excitement of heightened heartbeat while experiencing fear in a safe environment and can test their survival instinct when being propelled to the earth at high speed or turning suddenly in a new direction. In turn, a thrill seeker can also enjoy the feeling of peace when sitting on the shores of a lake watching a sunset. We can enjoy both.

This is a simple example, yet it asks us to be willing to get out of our comfort zone.

Through a variety of life experiences, whether pleasurable or painful, we add to our Emotional Palette and develop a depth of emotions that contribute to a richer understanding of ourselves and others and increase our empathy.

With 300 years, there would be plenty of time to venture outward, even if only taking small steps. If you failed at a new venture, you could learn from it and try another one. Not every attempt would have to have a perfect outcome. The excitement of discovery would be its reward. As has been said, "It is the journey, not the destination."

Instead of thinking, "I learned these things and I am close to the end of my life," how about thinking, "I have all this knowledge and wisdom now; how can I use them for the next phase of my life?" Life is not over till it's over.

# Chapter 11 Reflections

Our fear and uncertainty about the future can be paralyzing. No one really knows what the future will bring. Being afraid of the unknown is natural. We want to feel confident and safe at all times. As part of our evolutionary process, we must be willing to move forward and face unfamiliar situations. Through experience, we develop our inner wisdom. We discover that overcoming fear, or learning from our failures, are opportunities for us to gain new insights. They allow us to progress forward on our walk of life.

*Describe a time when you overcame one of your fears.*
*What did you learn from it?*

*What old fears can you release today that will allow you*
*to move forward and live a more fulfilling life?*

✦　✦　✦

# Enjoying Life through Food and Music

# Enjoying Life through Food and Music

Food is one of my great pleasures in life! It is interesting to discover how each region combines local crops to create delectable dishes. A simple dish can be enhanced with herbs and spices. Even something as basic as bread is made in so many different ways: American artisan breads, French baguette, Indian naan bread, Middle Eastern flat bread, Belgian waffles, Mexican tortillas, focaccia from Italy, bagels, rye bread, corn bread in the southern United States, banana bread, English muffins, fry bread, and many more. There are so many dishes to discover and enjoy! Sharing food creates a sense of community and connection between cultures.

Often during a meal or afterwards, when people retire for conversation, music is playing in the background. When I lived in Nashville, music was a favorite opportunity to bring folks together, "playing in the round," in the town's living rooms. Songwriters and musicians told stories in their unique ways. I learned to appreciate true country music there, with its roots in the southern states, Tennessee, West Virginia, and Texas.

When visiting New Orleans, I heard Dixieland Jazz and Cajun songs with local dialect. In Belgium and France, there was the traditional *la chanson française*. In my short life so far, I have been carried away by a variety of popular music: big band, blues, jazz, rock 'n' roll, rap, heavy metal, and more. In 300 years, it is certain that music will continue to be transformed. There is no stopping the evolution of music! How long can we keep saying, "I only love the music I grew up with"? We would learn to appreciate its many expressions, in the same way we do with the classics. Imagine all the music we'd experience in 300 years!

It all comes back to people and cultures and the spirit that drives them into the future. If I lived 300 years, I would discover many other interesting cultures.

# CHAPTER 12 REFLECTIONS

It's a great big world out there! It's hard to imagine all the cultures that inhabit the Earth. Each of them is made of people who have developed over the millennia. It is fascinating to think of how all these civilizations have evolved, creating their own food and music.

**What are your favorite foods? Why? Have you tried any new foods lately?**

**What kind of music do you like? Have you always enjoyed the same kind, or do you listen to a variety?**

**What can you do today to broaden your experience of people, food, music, and culture?**

✦ ✦ ✦

# Political and Social Instability

# Political and Social Instability

I learned about the effects of political instability through accounts that two women shared with me during the course of my work.

One day when I worked at the insurance company, I started to speak with a girl from our typing pool. I usually would say hi to her when I passed by. She was quiet and reserved, always keeping to herself.

On this day, I stopped and sat with her as she was sitting alone during lunch. We began to talk and became quick friends. Curious about her Asian background, I asked her where she was born and how she had come to live in Dallas, Texas. What she told me was shocking, coming from my quiet, unassuming new friend. She had grown up in South Vietnam in a modest family. She had gone to school and graduated with advanced studies in Business and English. She then found employment at the United States Embassy in Saigon as part of the office support personnel. She went on to tell me about an event that would change her life.

She was working at the US Embassy in Saigon as an office clerk on April 30, 1975. Although the Vietnam War was raging full force throughout the country, she felt relatively safe in the capital. She had gone to work just like a normal day. She lived at her parent's home, along with her brother and sister.

When she arrived at the Embassy, things were becoming chaotic. There was talk that the communist forces were advancing south and were expected to march into the capitol soon. For several weeks now, American personnel had started to evacuate throughout the country. As the day progressed, news was becoming dire. The People's Army of Vietnam had started to enter the city.

An emergency evacuation of the Embassy was called. She was given one hour to call her family and try to have them meet her there. US helicopters started to land on the roof of the building, where there was a small landing pad. She spoke to her family on the phone, telling them to quickly come to the embassy for the evacuation. She waited for them but they were not able to reach her. There was now chaos in the streets. Finally, it was her turn to leave. She climbed up the staircase leading to the rooftop helicopter pad and was among the lucky who were rescued that day.

When she arrived in the US, she was eventually provided employment with this insurance company in Dallas, Texas. For the following years after the fall of Saigon, she tried to locate her family but without success. She does not know what ever happened to them.

I was shocked and stunned by Mai's story. Here she was living alone in this country, having lost ties with her parents and siblings, not knowing if they would ever be reunited. I was reminded that we never know the suffering that others endure as they go about their ordinary lives.

Another time, I was managing a hotel, doing relief work in North Palm Beach, Florida. One day as I was walking on the property, I passed a room and noticed that the door was open. I looked inside and saw one of my housekeepers sitting on the bed sobbing. I walked in and asked her why she was crying. She didn't say anything for a while. Then she said to me that her cousin who lived in Haiti tried to come here. He got on a boat with others who were trying to come to America to find a better life. On the way, the boat capsized, and he drowned.

There were many stories like it on the news around that time. The poverty and oppressive political system in Haiti prompted many Haitians to make that perilous journey by sea to the United States. Often, hundreds of Haitian migrants would be packed on small boats headed to Florida. Many did not make it.

I do not know how we find hope in the midst of tragedy. Maybe with the belief that better days will come in the future. Perhaps, as Viktor Frankl said in Man's Search for Meaning, his account of his experience in Nazi death camps during the Second World War, although we cannot avoid suffering, we can choose to find meaning in it, and find purpose in it. For him, some days, the sight of a blade of grass rising through the snow-covered ground would bring him delight. Could I trust that I could move forward and find strength to reach ahead? I would want to remember that I would need to find meaning in the difficult experiences of my life, whether I lived one day or 300 years.

✦ ✦ ✦

# CHAPTER 13 REFLECTIONS

We each have our own perspective of the world, based on our individual life experiences. As we progress through life, we are molded by how we choose to react to these experiences, and we develop our beliefs and values. Social changes and world events also affect us. Let us examine our resilience to those changes in our lives.

**What challenges have you dealt with in your life?**
**How did you cope with them?**

**Of the social changes you have seen in your life, which have influenced you the most?**

**What possibilities might open up for you that were out of your reach in the past?**

✦ ✦ ✦

# PART III

# THE
# TRANSITIONAL
# GENERATION

# THE TRANSITIONAL GENERATION

# Considering Our Extended Lives

Now, allow me to muse a little, as I consider the possibility of us extending our lifespans. What if we could really live to be 150 or 200 years, as mentioned in a previous chapter? How would we be impacted personally and socially? We would be the Transitional Generation, the generation that would have to re-examine our beliefs about what we have been taught to expect from our lives, and to now consider a new life filled with new opportunities.

I was recently sitting in a circle with a focus group of people in their 70s and 80s. I posed to them the question of how they would feel about the prospect of living 150 to 200 years. These were their observations. (Their names have been changed to protect privacy.)

"Steve" commented, "We would have accrued wisdom to share. Having knowledge of the past, along with our life experience, we have much to teach now. We have become wiser, better people. If we could continue into this new phase of living, we would have much to contribute to a new generation, working hand in hand, creating a new future."

"Tom" confessed that he had learned humility "from the mistakes and dumb things I've done. I recognize that I'm not infallible."

Some other qualities gained were empathy, compassion, and patience. "Sally" mentioned how she looked back at the relationships that she had during her life, some that she had supported, others that she had harmed. She had grown wiser from her interactions with others.

"Mary" jumped in and said, "I have learned to forgive others for hurts they may have caused me. I've also had to let go of attachments to past losses. "

"Harold," an engineer, said, "We would have to keep our skills up, changing our careers and interests. If we chose to work the same career for a long time, we would see it evolve."

I asked him, "How might you see it evolve, and how would you adapt?"

"I may have to learn to evolve along with it," he said, learning or updating my skills, or I may decide to do something new and explore new interests. I would be required to be flexible, forward moving in my thinking, keeping in step with the changing times."

"Mary" then added, "We would have to learn to deal with change."

"Margaret" observed: "The pace of life doesn't have to be so darn fast! (I'm glad I'm slowing down.) I'd like to be more intentional about what I want to take on moving forward." She shared how her life, looking back, appeared to have been a constant rush, rush, rush, to get things done.

"Amy," who had been quiet so far, then asked: "What would be the financial cost of living an extended life? Could we afford to support ourselves?"

Amy's comment started the group discussing the social impacts of having a population with an extended lifespan. It may require us to re-examine our conception of retirement and social security. If we enjoy the benefits of a healthy extended lifespan, we will want to continue working. We will find fulfillment through meaningful occupations.

"Harold" said: "How about the environment, ecosystem, and the weather, what will the world look like? We would certainly feel a greater sense of urgency to maintain a healthy planet if we had a vested interest in its outcome and our future life in it."

"Mary" added: "What about the birth rate? If people lived that long would there be a need for population control? What about all the cars? Would our form of transportation change? Will we 'beam people up' like on Star Trek? Will we do away with airplanes and live in communities within walking distance from everything?"

Some spiritual subjects came up.

"Bill," who had not spoken yet, said: "We are here for a purpose, to learn lessons. These are decisions made by the Soul, how long we live on Earth."

Questions about reincarnation were also posed.

"Is it the end or do we return again?" asked Amy.

"Margaret" added, "I'm tired of being me, change is not easy. I want to be reborn anew."

"Pete," who had been listening to the conversation said, "We are eternal anyway. To reinvent ourselves, to continue our personal growth, either here, or in the hereafter, is an ongoing process."

"Steve" then observed, "I didn't know what it would be like to be 80— the perspective I have now, reflecting on my life, the wisdom gained. I enjoy nature now, write, and am more thoughtful. It seems alarming to realize that I've become an elder. I still feel young, although my body doesn't."

"Yes, Steve," I observed, "our perception of ourselves may change throughout the years, yet inside, we are still there, viewing the world around us."

I asked the group, "Eventually we will be approaching the end of a long life. Whether we live into our 70s, 80s or beyond, we will all have to face the reality of death. How do you feel about it?"

"Margaret" then said, "It's natural to die. The cycle of life and death: there is a sense of structure and security in that."

✦  ✦  ✦

Again, no one has had to really think about longevity before!!! We now have to consider our extended lives, and considering this sooner rather than too late in the game seems necessary. More than aging to 100, we now must consider how to do this gracefully, fully consciously, knowing that we will be active longer than past generations ever had to consider.

We would have to assume, as was the case with the centenarians, that we would be in good health to live that long. If we focus on staying healthy, we will be able to benefit from the advances that are here now and also on the horizon. We would re-examine our attitude about ourselves and about how we view the future. We would consider the quality of our lives moving forward, working fulfilling careers, exploring new activities, remaining curious with the "beginner's mind" and seeing the world with fresh eyes.

The thought of extending our lives by possibly an extra 100 years may feel daunting to some. Society's expectations are all around us. Our lives have already been mapped and we have followed the plan. First, when we are young, we are told, "You have your whole life ahead of you! The sky's the limit!" and we feel invincible. Then we begin school, learn to read and write and are exposed to the world beyond our families. By the time we reach high school, we begin to think about our future, the career we will choose, and the preparations required for achieving it. After high school, we may have gotten a job or gone to college or trade school, after which we went to work. Some others may choose another path and work as customer service agents, warehouse workers, or sales. Eventually, we are expected to marry, have children, buy a home, and spend a lot of time paying for it all. We may save money for our children's future education and for our eventual retirement. It will all happen very quickly. Society has already made arrangements for us to retire at 65-70 and collect Social Security and Medicare. These social structures have formed our attitudes and expectations about our futures. The reality of how our life unfolds may not be that smooth. Social Security does not provide enough money for retirement and many older people have to keep working. Some others may be bankrupt by medical debt. That is the reality today for many of us.

The Transitional Generation would have to re-examine its current beliefs. With our extended health and lifespan, we would have to take a new view of our future. We would have to change our ideas, such as, when I retire (from this job that I am tired of) I will be able to do the things that I've always wanted to do (such as travel, buy a boat, or begin a new hobby.) Instead, we would realize that our life is about finding ways to live life to the fullest, now. Not settling for unsatisfying employment, but instead, having an occupation that allows us to thrive as human beings.

To live in a society where an elder's insight, knowledge, and understanding is valued, where personal development is encouraged, will benefit the whole of society.

A final comment with respects to longevity and living responsibly was made by Steve in our focus group: "If we had to live in the world that we are creating, we may feel prompted to find solutions to its problems."

# CHAPTER 14 REFLECTIONS

Let us imagine that we are actually able to live to be 150 or 200 years old: we each have access to this medical breakthrough, it is safe, we are healthy, and we are looking at an extended future that we can share with our family and friends. Paraphrasing Joseph Campbell, how would you follow your bliss?

**Considering your future, what would you like to do? Would you continue with what you are doing now?**

**What is your attitude about yourself and your future?**

**Do you have a fresh outlook when exploring something that is new?**

**Do you have the "beginner's mind?"**

✦　✦　✦

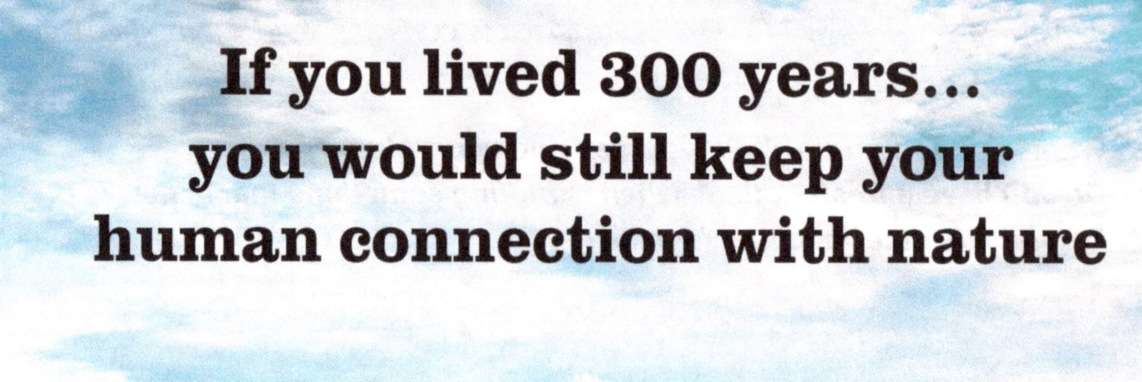

If you lived 300 years...
you would still keep your
human connection with nature

# CHAPTER 15
# Our Connection with Nature

While it is exciting to think of future advances in technology, we must still remember to keep our balance by interacting with the natural world. It has sustained us in the past. If we become part of the transitional generation, we must continue to maintain our human connection with nature, as well as preserve it for future generations. We feel enlivened when we go for a walk by a lake or ocean, or on a trail in the forest or on a mountain.

Strolling in the woods, we are surrounded with the fragrant smell of trees, the sounds of the leaves rustling and birds chirping, the feeling under our feet as we are walking on the earth. We feel our bond with the life force that surrounds us.

By the ocean, we feel its mist on our faces as the surf crashes up against the rocks. Walking on its shore, we may notice seashells on the sand and hear the cry of seagulls flying overhead. At the end of the day, we may enjoy watching a sunset with its kaleidoscope of vibrant colors.

These are only a few ways that nature reminds us of our humanity and replenishes our soul. We are a part of it, and it is the source of our beginnings. Even with a short life, we should be visiting nature regularly.

◆　◆　◆

# CHAPTER 15 REFLECTIONS

We are connected to nature, so it is important to remember that we cannot live without it. Whether we enjoy nature by simply going outside for a walk, or whether we choose to become environmental activists, nature is an integral part of our lives. In the next 300 years, we will need to become good stewards of our planet and keep a watchful eye on its well-being.

If you enjoy watching films about nature, earth sciences, and astronomy, sharing them with children can foster an awareness of our great world.

***Are you able to appreciate some quality time with nature, or do the demands of everyday make it difficult to schedule it into your calendar? How could you make time with nature?***

**Think of a time when you have enjoyed being around nature. How did it make you feel?**

**How do you think it improves the quality of your life when you make time for nature?**

✦　✦　✦

IF YOU LIVED 300 YEARS . . .

YOU MAY HAVE TO CHANGE
YOUR PERSPECTIVE

MORE THAN ONCE

Change
your thoughts
and you
will change
your world

# What the Future Holds

No one knows what our futures hold for us. No one knows how long we will live. How do you deal with uncertainty? Can you look at the future, living with resilience, curious to see what you may find beyond the next ridge? Who are your role models? How have they inspired you? These are the questions you may ask yourself if you are ready to grasp life like an arrow and allow it to carry you into the future.

One of my dreams is to someday fly in space. It is not so far-fetched of an idea anymore. Commercial opportunities are being offered now—at a high price of course—with the opportunity to experience weightlessness while orbiting the Earth in a spacecraft. Ah, to be able to view our beautiful planet from above! I would love to take photos from the craft's window. In 1971, astronaut Edgar Mitchell was fundamentally changed when he viewed our magnificent planet upon his return flight from the moon in Apollo 14. He experienced a strong sense of connectedness with the universe and later founded the Institute of Noetic Sciences, promoting scientific research into the nature of consciousness. Some day in the not-too-far future, I believe space will be a travel destination for everyone.

That will change our perspective on a personal level. It will give us a greater sense of kinship and allow for a unified humanity.

If I live long enough, I may learn how time and consciousness are related. Maybe a researcher will solve my riddle.

Although I have played with the idea of living 300 years throughout this book, I envy the future generations that will benefit even more than us from the research in longevity. This book is for them also, that they may grow into an inspiring Future Generation.

✦　✦　✦

# CHAPTER 16 REFLECTIONS

We have a responsibility to hold hope for the future. With hope, we look for solutions to the world's difficulties. With hope, we create new innovations that can benefit others. With hope, we can dream of new possibilities and find ways to make them come to pass. It is up to us to dream of a boundless future for all to enjoy.

**What dream have you entertained about your future?**

**If you could accomplish anything, without the prospect of failure, what would it be?**

**If you could pass on your wisdom to future generations, what would you share with them?**

# CONCLUSION

Seize the day!

# CONCLUSION
# Seize the Day!

I must sound as though I've had a mostly idyllic life, the way I appear to have taken control of my life. However, I believe that much happened out of luck or synchronicity and being open to new opportunities. Keeping an open mind allowed for creativity to unfold. I had no control over my adoption shortly after birth, over being introduced to nature by my father, over ending my dance classes. Yet, these events opened new opportunities for me: going to Europe at the age of 17, pursuing the arts later in life, and being willing to reinvent myself many times over. All these experiences taught me much about myself. As one of the elders in the focus group said, I have learned humility from some of the mistakes and dumb things I have done, and as another said, I have grown wiser from my interactions with others.

◆　◆　◆

I could not end this without mentioning another aspect of making life choices that I considered. Although I like to plan and work towards a goal, there is another element involved that I've always been aware of. It is a feeling or nudge that there is sometimes something I'm supposed to do. I know when that feeling comes up. The thing I'm supposed to do; should do; that is really important that I do is not always the easy thing to do at the time. When I follow that prompt, when I make the hard decision, perhaps to walk away from the familiar, and am willing to move towards the unknown that is calling me, I have been blessed in immeasurable ways that I could never have anticipated. Each one of those special choices I made has greatly enriched my life experience.

However, I also had many unexpected and difficult experiences along the way. They are part of living a full life. Over the years, I have overcome many adversities, as well as a series of health issues and injuries. As a woman, I've experienced discrimination and at times, lack of opportunity. I've been rich and poor. I've hired others to serve me and have served others. If you live long enough, life will happen to you. No one is unscathed by life's experiences. Some bad things will happen. But also, there is a lot of good in the world. If you dare to grasp the good, then the world has much to offer.

I am grateful for all the events of my life: my birth to an unwed mother, the opportunities I received from my adoptive family, the many careers that I've had, the many places in the world that I have visited, and most of all, the people I have known. I am a better person today because of them.

I am an optimist and believe that I can achieve much if I choose to try. I've lived in hot weather and cold weather, in the mountains, in the desert, and by the sea. I did it all by choice. Each time, I met wonderful people who I learned from. I discovered new ways to be of service to those in need. Most of all, I realized over and over how much we have in common. We all want to feel loved and live a happy life.

Go forward with life! It has so many wonders to reveal. Even if you lived 300 years, it still wouldn't be enough to discover them all.

✦　✦　✦

# PHOTO ATTRIBUTIONS

All photos and illustrations used in creating the book are from Canva graphic design platform and free to use. The author chooses to recognize photos and illustrations used with attributions to recognize the artists. Compositions are created by the author.

Cover Photo: Future by RBFried from Getty Images Signature.

Chapter 1: Natural Background by jakubgojda.

Chapter 2: MADA3GTnauo-1672530853319.jpg; Close-up Shot of Two People by Gabriel Tapia from Pexels; country road for background by Thanapol sinsrang from Getty Images Pro.

Chapter 3: 2167549.jpg by Berzin from pixabay; World water day concept by Boonyachoat from Getty Images; Art concept by alexis84 from Getty Images; Music concept by SergeyNivens from Getty Images; Horses at horse farm by volgariver from Getty Images Pro.

Chapter 4: Business Travel by Maksymowicz from Getty Images; Chinese Lanterns by L3ankadi from Getty Images; Close Up of Vintage Photo by Susanne Jutzeler from Pexels; 6649544.jpg be MemoryCatcher from pixabay; Old Town of Warsaw by Skitterphoto from pixabay.

Chapter 5: Red Poppy Flowers by janske@janske.

Chapter 6: Working by Proxy Tiatanan from Getty Images; Working in factory by shironosov from Getty Images Pro; Designer at work by shironosov from Getty Images Pro; Working by MarijaRadovic from Getty Images.

Chapter 7: Happy Black and White Cartoon by Lineartestpilot; Businessman Entrepreneur by dvgstock; Black and White Cartoon Trumpet by Lineartsetpilot2: Black and White Cartoon Kite by Lineartestpilot2; line graphic elements in canva.

Chapter 8: Art Concept by halfpoint.

Chapter 9: Starry Night Sky by Nikiko from pixabay.

Chapter 10: Stress Balls by TwaN from TwaN's Images.

Chapter 11: Young Friends on Thrilling Ride by Jacob Lund@jacoblund.

Chapter 12: Food Desserts by Trang Doan from Pexels; Man Playing Cello by piotreku2 from pixabay; assorted india food cuisine by margouillatphotos from Getty Images Pro; 2571955.jpg by StockSnap from pixabay; Plated Food by Alexy Almond from Pexels; Asian Meals on the Table by karriezhu from pixabay; 3202707.jpg by SocialButterflyMMG from pixabay.

Chapter 13: Group of People on Street by Romina Ordonez from Pexels; photos from canva.

Chapter 14: Background by studiobest.

Chapter 15: Person Standing on Top of ... by Archie Binamira from Pexels.

Chapter 16: Blue Planet Earth by DAPA Images; Change your Thoughts by mareculiasz from Getty Images; photos from canva.

Conclusion: Happy People by alphaspirit from Getty Images Pro.

# Paula Forget

Paula Forget developed a personal philosophy in her early 20's, after exploring the outlook of centenarians, of how to live with resilience in changing times. It evolved naturally, encouraging her to live a life of optimism, curiosity and wonder. She has had careers in several fields including the airlines, insurance, hospitality, fine arts, and teaches mindfulness meditation.

She promotes a purpose-filled life, self-inquiry, and personal development.

Visit www.ifyoulived300years.com for more information.